BURIAL OR CREMATION:

Does It Matter?

Donald Howard

THE BANNER OF TRUTH TRUST

THE BANNER OF TRUTH TRUST
3 Murrayfield Road, Edinburgh EH12 6EL, UK
P.O. Box 621, Carlisle, PA 17013, USA

*

© Donald Howard 2001

ISBN 0 85151 803 6

*

Typeset in 11/13 pt Sabon MT
Printed in Great Britain by
Howie & Seath,
Edinburgh

Burial or Cremation:
Does It Matter?

'We are here to commit the body . . . to the ground, earth to earth, ashes to ashes, dust to dust . . . '[1]

This once familiar sentence is heard less and less. In fact, so few are being buried today that the words seem doomed to oblivion – cremation is the way to go in the western world. There are many arguments in its favour: the ceremony is brief and simple; the bereaved are spared both the expense of grave maintenance and the temptation to give morbid veneration to a grave site. An Australian funeral director probably spoke for the modern generation when he said that a mobile population means that there is less of the 'go-back-to-the-grave syndrome'. But the overwhelming practical reason for cremation is that it saves using valuable real estate. These arguments are valid but have one common feature: none is biblically based. Whatever the question before them, Christians should submit to the authority of the Bible and not rely upon pragmatic arguments. We must always ask, 'Does the Bible have anything to say about this?' The answer to this question will determine not only how we dispose of the bodies of our loved ones but also the directions we give for our own departure.

[1] *The Order for the Burial of the Dead* in the *Book of Common Prayer*.

Such a personal matter makes it easy for subjective reasons to cloud our judgment. People are influenced (albeit unconsciously) by memories of loved ones who were cremated or buried, with an understandable desire to have their remains 'united in death'. The feelings are real and call for gracious counsel, but always God's Word is the Christian's arbiter, not a personal or traditional view.

Many think that they are taking the high spiritual ground when they adopt a cavalier attitude to the disposal of the body (their own or that of anyone else) with relative indifference. 'When I'm gone, they can do what they like with me – I won't be here.' Again, we must look to our final authority.

Supporters of cremation regard the lack of specific direction as permitting them to make their own decision. But burial alone has the endorsement of God's Word, and that Word, not tradition, sentiment or custom must direct us in both our living and our dying.

It is the writer's firm belief that burial alone gives specific testimony to the Christian doctrine of the resurrection of the dead.

A History of Burial

The three great national exceptions to burning the body in the ancient world were China, Egypt and Israel. The Chinese held it as part of their moral code that the bodies of the dead should be buried in China's earth. As a small girl, my mother used to spend time in her father's produce store in Sydney's George Street North. He had won the respect of the many Chinese seamen who called into port, mainly by witnessing their signatures as a Justice of the Peace. My mother could recall how they would often bring empty coffins from China to their countrymen living in Australia. These were kept as a solemn reminder of their ultimate death and the obligation to transport their bodies back to their homeland.

The Chinese saw the need to have a tangible link in death with the soil from which they had sprung. Although the practice had some correspondence with the biblical point of view, the evil of it was that it was associated with ancestor worship. Some critics of the Chinese custom claimed that it penalized the living because a deep veneration caused the best spots of land to be reserved for the burial of the dead.[1]

The Egyptians left vast numbers of tomb pictures and papyrus records which tell of embalming and burial in Egypt. As Genesis draws to its close, Joseph orders the Egyptian physicians to embalm his father Israel. 'So the physicians embalmed him, taking a full forty days, for that was the time required for embalming. And the Egyptians mourned him for seventy days' (*Gen.* 50:28).

Embalming was obviously a sophisticated process. By the Eighteenth Dynasty (a period beginning a century or two after Jacob's death), it normally took seventy days. Significantly, the mourning for Jacob was very little short of the seventy-two days observed for a Pharaoh.[2]

According to J. Vergote, embalmers and physicians were members of distinct professions. Joseph probably chose the physicians to avoid the magico-religious rites of the professional embalmers.[3]

Not only was there a probable significance in the embalming being done by physicians, but the burial itself

---

[1] S. M. Houghton, 'Earth to earth': Considerations on the practice of cremation, *Banner of Truth*, July/August 1969, p. 37.

[2] Von Rad, *Joseph en Egypte*, cited in Derek Kidner, *Genesis*, London: Tyndale Press, 1967, p. 222.

[3] Cited in Kidner, *Genesis*, p. 223.

was in stark contrast to Egyptian custom. There was none of the superstitious ritual such as food for the journey into the next world as seen in the tombs and pyramids of Joseph's day, and certainly no elaborate edifice. The reason was that by the time of Joseph's death, a tradition had been established amongst the Hebrew people, and Joseph was concerned that it be followed.

Old Testament Foundation

The first death recorded in the Bible is that of Abel who was slain by his brother Cain. With fire readily available, burning would have enabled Cain to conceal his crime, but he apparently either left the body where it was or gave it some sort of burial. All that the Bible says is that God told him, 'The voice of your brother's blood cries to me from the ground' (*Gen.* 4:10).

The only information on death in following generations is the phrase, 'and he died'.

The first specific reference to burial is when Abraham negotiates with the local inhabitants to bury his wife Sarah (*Gen.* 23). Abraham starts by telling the Hittites that he is a stranger and sojourner among them (verse 4). The stranger is a foreigner in a strange land possessing no property and having no fixed habitation. 'Sojourner' means almost 'squatter' – one with a dwelling but not property in the form of land. Abraham can class himself as both of these. Sometimes he settles down; sometimes he wanders as a nomad. His reference to his status recalls especially the fact that he does not as yet possess any land in this country.[1]

[1] H. C. Leupold, *Exposition of Genesis*, London: Evangelical Press, 1972, p. 643.

The purchase of a plot by Abraham was testimony to his absolute faith in God's promises. It was not, as some feel, an option on the whole; his title rested upon God's covenant, not upon any such device as a legal purchase agreement. When Abraham dies, Isaac and Ishmael bury him with Sarah, in 'the field which Abraham purchased from the children of Heth' (*Gen*. 23:19).

The letter to the Hebrews gives us the true perspective: 'These all died in faith' (*Heb*. 11:13). How do we know? They left their bones in Canaan, a witness to the promise made clear in Joseph's dying words, 'God will surely remember you, and you shall carry up my bones from here' (*Gen*. 50:25). Calvin's comment is pertinent: 'While they themselves were silent . . . the sepulchre cried aloud, that death formed no obstacle to their entering on the possession of it.'[1]

As we study the burial of Abraham's descendants, it is interesting that the report of Ishmael's death makes no mention of burial. This is not to say that he died without faith, but that he had no stake in the promised land and laid no claim to it by a reported burial (*Gen*. 25:17).

By contrast, there is specific reference to the burial of Jacob. As his death drew near in Egypt, 'He charged (his sons) and said unto them: "I am about to be gathered unto my people; bury me with my fathers in the cave that is in the field of Ephron the Hittite [note the recurring emphasis on Abraham's purchase from the Hittites] . . . There they buried Abraham and Sarah his wife; there they buried Isaac and Rebekah his wife; and there I buried Leah." ' (*Gen*. 49:29–31). Joseph did not ask to be buried there. The oath which Joseph caused his brothers to swear was that they would take the coffin containing his bones from Egypt (*Gen*. 50:25). Just

[1] Cited in Kidner, *Genesis*, p. 145.

as his father Jacob had insisted on being carried back to the promised land for burial, so Joseph made his relatives swear that they would perform the like service for him.

Other writers such as Philo and Josephus enlarge on Joseph's fortitude and his wisdom; the Psalmist tells of his imprisonment when 'the word of the LORD tried him' (*Psa.* 105:19). But the writer of Hebrews singles out one incident only to illustrate his trust in God's covenant: 'By faith Joseph, when his end was near, spoke about the exodus of the Israelites from Egypt and gave instructions about his bones' (*Heb.* 11:22).

Apart from his earlier teens, Joseph had spent the whole of his long life in Egypt; but Egypt was not his home. Even when the rest of his family came down to Egypt at his invitation, he knew that their residence there would be but temporary. So presumably his coffin was kept in the house of one of his descendants in the land of Goshen for the next four-hundred-odd years. (Imagine each successive generation querying the reason for retaining such a macabre piece of furniture!)

As the bondage worsened, that coffin was a mute guarantee of their future redemption, the Exodus. For forty years in the wilderness they carried those bones to the promised land. The book of Joshua does not close until Joseph's bones are buried in Shechem according to his command (*Josh.* 24:32).

Growing Anticipation

From this time on, burial was the norm and of increasing significance for God's people as they came to regard the body with increasing reverence.

Towards the end of the forty years following the flight from Egypt, Aaron died and was buried in the wilderness (*Deut.* 10:6) His death before entering the Promised Land was a judgment upon his own sin of disobedience at Meribah – a contrast with many illustrious descriptions of his role as Israel's first high priest.

Numbers records adds that 'he was gathered to his people' (*Num*. 20:26). Wenham points out that this was the usual description of death in old age for a righteous man.[1] These words were also used of Abraham, Ishmael, Isaac, Jacob and Moses.

Moses climbed Pisgah and died alone, but so important was the disposal of his body that he was buried by the LORD himself (*Deut*. 34:5–6).

By way of contrast, to be left unburied and not be 'gathered' was a fearful mark of divine judgment. Jeremiah writes of 'those slain by the LORD', that 'They will not be mourned or gathered up or buried, but will be like refuse lying on the ground' (*Jer*. 25:33; compare 15:3, 16:4–6 and 22:18–19).

That is why shortly after the burial of Aaron, the Midianites who had treated the Israelites as enemies and deceived them were denied proper burial (*Num*. 25:4). It appears that their bodies were impaled and publicly displayed.[2]

The Moabites, with whom they were closely associated, were judged by the LORD because they burned, rather than buried, their enemy the king of Edom (*Amos* 2:1).

Conversely, the men of Jabesh Gilead were commended by David for their bravery in retrieving the bodies of Saul and his sons from where they were fastened to the wall of Beth Shan and burying them (*2 Sam*. 2:5). David refers to their action as 'this kindness and faithfulness' – a reminder that the proper burial of the dead had always been regarded in Judaism as an act of true piety.[3]

---

[1] Gordon J. Wenham, *Numbers* (*Tyndale Old Testament Commentaries*), Leicester: IVP, 1993, p. 153.

[2] See discussion in Wenham, *Numbers*, p. 186.

[3] S. Goldman, *Samuel*, London: Soncino Press, 1977, p. 193.

So persistently was this belief held by God's people that Nehemiah's burden for Jerusalem in ruins was accentuated by the realization that it was 'the city where my fathers are buried' (*Neh.* 2:5). The way that the people of Israel treated the body after death was an expression of their faith. Abraham's only hope in life was God's promise that the very soil on which he trod and where he buried Sarah was one day to be his. His descendants held to this promise. Yet the writer to the Hebrews says that they were longing for a better country – a heavenly one (*Heb.* 11:6).

Slowly the realization of the certainty of life beyond the grave came, and the hope always centred upon the body. 'Multitudes who sleep in the dust of the earth will awake: some to everlasting life, others to shame and everlasting contempt' (*Dan.* 12:2). Whenever a resurrection life is mentioned in the Old Testament, it comes through the revivifying of the body of flesh left behind: 'But your dead will live; their bodies will rise. You who dwell in the dust, wake up and shout for joy!' (*Isa.* 26:19).

So it was that after the death of Lazarus, his sister Martha replies to Jesus' words on resurrection by saying, 'I know he will rise again in the resurrection at the last day' (*John* 11:24).

New Testament Realization

Resurrection of the body is the unique teaching of the Christian faith. It is with the resurrection of the Lord Jesus Christ that the doctrine finds full expression. John's gospel describes seven miracles of Jesus as 'signs'. The term is significant in that it does not dwell on the divine power at Jesus' disposal, but, like a sign, each miracle points to a deeper reality beyond itself. The first was at Cana when Jesus turned water to wine (*John* 2); the last in Bethany where he raised Lazarus from the dead (*John* 11).

This climactic sign pointed to Jesus' imminent rising from the dead. When Jesus heard Mary's traditional Jewish belief in a general resurrection he replied with the grandest affirmation of all history: 'I am the resurrection and the life. He who believes in me, though he dies, yet shall he live, and whoever lives and believes in me shall never die' (*John* 11:25).

Jesus did not mean that the believer would not die physically. Lazarus had died before he spoke these words, and millions of Jesus' followers have died since – as shall we, if our time arrives before his triumphant return. But the death of believers has no eternal significance. They do not die with reference to the age to come. It was on the basis of his soon-to-come resurrection that Martha believed. Her faith is not a vague, formless credulity. It had content, and doctrinal content at that.[1] Her faith was to be vindicated within a short period when Jesus himself would rise and guarantee the resurrection of all who put their trust in him as Lord.

The death, burial and resurrection of Jesus are the three historic climactic events upon which our salvation depends. They stand at the heart of the gospel. Produce the bones of Jesus and the whole Christian church will crumble. Paul is emphatic: 'I delivered unto you first of all [that is, as of prime importance] that which I also received, that Christ died for our sins according to the scriptures, that he was buried and that he rose again on the third day according to the scriptures' (*1 Cor.* 15:3–4).

Before Jesus' resurrection came the cross, and between the cross and resurrection was the burial of our Lord's body. Jesus implied burial when he prophesied that on the third day he would rise again (*Matt.* 20:19); burial was explicit when, as

---

[1] Leon Morris, *The Gospel of John (New International Commentary on the New Testament)*, Grand Rapids: Eerdmans, 1971, p. 551.

Mary anointed his feet at Bethany, he stilled criticism of her action by saying that it was a preparation 'for the day of my burial' (*Matt.* 26:12). Shortly afterwards he looked to his approaching glorification: 'Unless a grain of wheat falls into the ground and dies, it remains a single seed' (*John* 12:24). Paul uses the same analogy when he reminds his readers that when 'wheat or some other grain' is sown, it brings forth its own kind (*1 Cor.* 15:37). Burning simply cannot fit into the analogy. Seed is not burned to germinate; it is sown into the ground. Burial of the body is an expression of faith in its later being raised in the same likeness.

Apart from doctrinal factors, the reason the early church held so strongly to burial was twofold: Jewish practice and the burial or our Lord.

After his death, Joseph of Arimathea approached Pilate (Mark says he went in 'boldly') and asked permission to bury Jesus' body (*John* 19:38).

Jews regarded proper burial of their dead as most important. Many went out of their way to see that their compatriots received proper burial, which may have influenced Joseph. When Pilate gave permission, Joseph took the body and with the help of Nicodemus, prepared it for burial (*John* 19:39–42). It is pedantic to say that the placing of a body in a tomb cut into rock is not a burial as it is not an earthen grave. Both the disciple who outran John and also Mary Magdalene 'bent over' to look into the empty tomb (*John* 20:5). In any case, some caves were vertical, with the stone lying on top; others horizontal, with the stone against the entrance as was probably here with the tomb of Jesus.[1]

On the last day, the same power which raised the body of Jesus from the tomb in a Jerusalem garden will raise believers'

[1] *Ibid*, p. 559.

bodies that they may be 'like unto his glorious body' (*Phil.* 3:21), while those of unbelievers shall be raised to shame and to everlasting contempt. The stress on burial in the death of Jesus was to ensure that his followers would accept the twin truths of his physical death and bodily resurrection.

In the words of Paul, 'If Christ has not been raised, your faith is futile; you are still in your sins. Then also those who have fallen asleep in Christ are lost. If only for this life we have hope in Christ, we are to be pitied more than all men' (*1 Cor.* 15:19). But he has been raised, thank God, and upon his death, burial and resurrection we base the certainty of our Christian hope (*Titus* 2:13).

Cremation's Origins

Most westerners believe that cremation of the body is comparatively modern, yet prior to Christianity it was almost universal among Indo-European people and in North America. Hindus have burned their dead for centuries and it is common amongst Buddhists. European tombs of the Stone and Bronze Ages testify to its prevalence. It was fashionable among ancient Greeks and Romans, particularly with the official and wealthier classes.[1]

In Virgil's *Aeneid*, the hero's body is burned on cypress logs, his ashes placed in an urn and sent home. Celtic and Aryan races all burned their dead.

Considerations of economy or convenience had a good deal to do with this choice in the Roman Empire. (So some of today's arguments are at least as old as Julius Caesar!) According to the Oxford Classical Dictionary, 'It does not appear that these two methods (cremation and inhumation) corresponded to different eschatological beliefs.'[2]

---

[1] Houghton, 'Earth to earth', p. 37–8.   [2] Cited by Houghton, p. 38

The striking feature is that the reasons for cremation among many ancient races, both primitive and civilized, were religious. Many thought departed spirits would return to buried bodies to plague the living; others that burning set the spirit free to enjoy unfettered bliss. Some Animists in Irian Jaya burn their dead, whilst to other tribes the very idea is repugnant.[1]

Perhaps the main indication that the basic factors in favour were religious, is that wherever Christianity spread, cremation ceased amongst the believers. According to Francis Schaeffer, the spread of Christianity in Europe can be established by studying the cemeteries: Romans burned their dead while Christians buried theirs.[2]

Christian burial was one further custom to accentuate the difference between believers and those around them. In itself it served as a protest against paganism and was recognised as such.

In 177 AD, heathen persecutors of the church at Lyons burned the martyrs' bodies and threw their ashes into the Rhône. 'This they did,' said contemporary records, 'as though they could overcome God and rob the martyrs of the new birth (of their bodies)'. They did it, as they say, 'that [the Christians] might have no hope of the resurrection, in the confidence of which they have introduced a new and strange religion amongst us, despising torments and ready to face death with joy. Now let us see whether they will rise again, and whether their God will help them and deliver them out of our hands.'[3]

---

[1] Thomas Reeve, former Agricultural Officer in New Guinea for twelve years, in correspondence with the author.

[2] *How Should We Then Live?* Wheaton, Illinois: Crossway, 1983.

[3] T. C. Hammond, *The New Creation*, London: Marshall, Morgan and Scott, 1953, p. 170.

The *Letter of the Churches* in Eusebius' *Ecclesiastical History* also describes how the martyrs of Lyons were scourged, thrown to wild beasts and burned. Those who suffocated in prison were given to the dogs. Witnesses wrote that the authorities 'kept a careful guard by night and day lest any should receive funeral rites. And then they actually exposed what the wild beasts and the fire had left behind – mangled or charred, as the case might be – and the heads of the others together with their severed trunks, and guarded them likewise from burial with a military watch for many days . . . We were plunged in great grief, in that we could not bury the bodies in the earth . . . In every possible way they kept guard, as if the prevention of burial would bring them great gain.'

The records tell how the bodies were exposed to the elements, burned, reduced to ashes and then swept into the Rhône so that not a trace might remain upon the earth. Such strong positions taken by Christians and pagans show how the heathen believed that by destruction of the body they could stop its resurrection, and the importance of the doctrine to the early church.[1] The heresy that burial or burning can affect the final judgment and destiny of the body is still held in the modern world. H. G. Wells, for example, believed that a martyr who was hanged and buried instead of being burned would benefit at the resurrection.[2]

Although this view crops up continually, it is not the issue. Neither in burning nor burial does the body continue in its earthly state; it is either destroyed by intense heat or it slowly disintegrates into the dust from which the first body came. After all, if the treatment of the body influenced its

[1] J. Stevenson, ed., *A New Eusebius*, London: SPCK, 1963, p. 41.
[2] Hammond, *The New Creation*, p. 169.

[15]

resurrection, what would happen to those who had been taken by sharks, bombed, buried at sea or otherwise disposed of?

Enlightened Christians have never been bothered by such thoughts. As far back as 234 AD, less than sixty years after the martyrs of Lyons were denied burial, Minucius Felix wrote, 'Do you think that if anything is withdrawn from our feeble eyes, it perishes to God? Every body, whether it is dried up into dust, or attenuated into smoke, is withdrawn from us, but it is reserved for God in the custody of the elements. Nor, as you believe, do we fear any loss from sepulture but we adopt the ancient and better custom of burying in the earth.'[1]

What the martyrdoms of Lyons and the observations of archaeologists cited by Schaeffer do prove is that within the first two centuries of the Christian era, burial was tenaciously held as the distinctive Christian custom. It remained so until well into the nineteenth century.

Biblical Burnings

Although burial was the historic practice amongst believers in the Old Testament, there are admittedly many reports of burnings. Between the Exodus and the Conquest, hundreds of people were burned in divine judgment.

Within a few days of leaving Sinai, the LORD's anger was kindled against those who began complaining and sowing dissension. 'Fire from the LORD burned among them and consumed some.' Only when Moses prayed to the LORD did the fire abate (*Num.* 11:1–3).

After the revolt of Korah, two hundred and fifty men who had assembled against Moses and Aaron were devoured by

[1] *Ibid.*, p. 171.

fire (*Num*. 16:35). Sexual intercourse between a man and his mother-in-law was to be punished by burning; the same end was pronounced on a priest's daughter who played the harlot (*Lev*. 20:14; 21:19). (Judah had intended the same punishment for Tamar until his own involvement was revealed (*Gen*. 38:24).

When Achan stole the items from Jericho which were under the divine ban, the LORD did not turn 'from the fierceness of his anger' until Achan and his family had been stoned to death and their bodies burnt before being buried under a pile of rocks (*Josh*. 7:25–26)

When the kingdom split centuries later, Jeroboam of the northern kingdom established the worship of a golden calf in Bethel and Dan. This was to prevent people continuing to sacrifice to the LORD in the temple of Jerusalem. But a 'man of God from Judah' prophesied that the bones of those priests conducting the forbidden worship would be burned during Josiah's reign (*1 Kings* 12:28 and 13:1). Not only did Josiah enact this judgment, he also 'desecrated Topheth . . . so no-one could use it to sacrifice his son or daughter in the fire to Molech' (*2 Kings* 23:10).

Nations outside Israel brought themselves under judgment for burning corpses. Amos pronounced the fire of judgment upon Moab because its king burned the bones of Edom's king (*Amos* 2:1). Rabbi Dr S. M. Lehrman comments that the sentence was not because of Moab's 'endless inroads and devastations of Israel, but for a deed of impiety, not otherwise known, against a king of Edom, Israel's foe.'[1]

Leviticus contains several edicts against offering one's children by fire; both Israelites or strangers associated with the pagan practice were warned that death by stoning would

---

[1] *The Twelve Prophets*, London: Soncino Press, 1979, p. 88.

be the sentence pronounced upon the guilty (*Lev.* 20:1–5). When the people of Judah resorted to the practice in Jeremiah's day, the LORD condemned them for 'such a detestable thing' (*Jer.* 32:35). As fire consumed the sacrifice offered in place of the sinner, so God's fire of judgment fell upon those guilty of such a hideous sin in God's sight.

Not all burnings were included under a blanket ban. The men of Jabesh-Gilead were commended for their bravery in recovering the bodies of King Saul and his sons and burning them to prevent further desecration by the Philistines (*1 Sam.* 31:11–13).

When men died in a house during Amos' time, it seems that burning was unusual, and, as we know from modern medicine, necessary to check infection. The reaction seems to have been one of concern for the plight of the bodies rather than there being any thought of judgment (*Amos* 6:10).

There are so many dead from the hosts of Gog and Magog in Ezekiel that it takes seven months to bury them (*Ezek.* 39:12). There is no mention of burning.

The New Testament contains only one reference to burning. This is in Paul's well known chapter on love where he stresses that even the laying down of one's life is futile unless motivated by love (*1 Cor.* 13:3).

Once again it needs to be reaffirmed that burning cannot defeat the will of God with regard to the eternal destiny of the body. It is of no consequence whether saints were burned during the Roman Empire's persecution or at the instigation of the Roman Catholic Church when 288 perished in England alone during the four years of Mary Tudor's reign.[1] Those who die in Christ shall reign with Christ. Nevertheless the symbol of fire as the ultimate evidence of God's wrath is as

[1] J. C. Ryle, *Five English Reformers*, London: Banner of Truth, 1960.

consistent in the New Testament as in the Old. What should be of great concern is that the most dreadful references comes from the lips of the Lord Jesus himself (for example, *Matt.* 13:42, 50; 18:8). We need to think both carefully and biblically before we subject the redeemed bodies of our loved ones to the agency of fire.

A Late Change

For over eighteen hundred years, cremation was never considered in countries which had experienced widespread gospel preaching or influence. Then in the 1870s a few Italian chemists and physicians appear to have initiated the modern movement – an irony when one considers that the Roman Catholic Church stood almost alone in its opposition to the process for the next hundred years.

In 1877, cremation was legalized in Italy, the charismatic leader Garibaldi being cremated five years later.

The first cremation society in England was formed in 1874, mainly through the efforts of the Professor of Surgery at London University, Sir Henry Thompson.

Land was purchased for a crematorium, but the Home Office was hostile to the scheme and for a time it remained in abeyance. In 1884 a father was indicted for attempting to burn the body of his child, instead of having it buried. The resultant legal judgment laid it down that the father's act was not an offence against English law, unless it could be proved that a public nuisance had been committed.

With this encouragement, the Cremation Society pushed ahead and in 1902 an Act of Parliament gave definite legalization to the practice. At the same time it exempted any clergyman from conducting such a service if he were opposed to the practice.

Sir Henry was first president of the society and strongly advocated cremation until his own death in 1904. A professed agnostic, he was the author of a short book entitled *The Unknown God*, taking his title from Paul's sermon in Athens. His book claimed that God was merely infinite and eternal energy, and that truth could be learned only through empirical observation by man's unaided efforts.

Thompson belittled revelation and divine authority. He regarded Christ as a remarkable teacher, but really no more than a young Jewish enthusiast. In Thompson's view, any person of reasonable education would eventually become agnostic and discard any teaching involving supernatural revelation. At his death there were ten crematoria in Britain. After his death, cremations gradually increased, reaching two thousand per annum in 1922.

It is interesting that while the ancients justified burning on theological grounds, as did early Christians in burying their dead, burning in modern Europe and Britain occurred within the context of strong assaults upon the Christian faith from secular philosophy and scientific materialism. Liberal theology had invaded the churches, and, though cause and effect cannot logically be established, spiritual regression and the progress of cremation ran parallel to each other. At the same time, belief in the resurrection of the body and of Christ himself was decreasing.

In this way, burial lost its significance for the simple reason that death spelled the end of the body – a belief which is a clear contradiction of Biblical teaching.

The Dignity of the Body

Christians through the ages have revered the body as God's creation – a body which shall one day be raised in changed form for eternal life with Christ, or for eternal punishment. This dignity of the body from a biblical perspective can be traced to man's creation as a reflection of the divine nature (*Gen.* 1:26) and to the body's eternal destiny.

All physical life is the product of God's creation; each form of life has a different body as it has pleased God (*1 Cor.* 15:38). When Christ took a human body it was perfect in every respect, being without sin (*Heb.* 4:15).

Despite having fallen, man still retains the impression of the divine image, blurred though it admittedly is. Our bodies are imperfect through sin, but the bodies of believers shall be raised in a perfected state. This gives dignity to the body, both in life and in death.

We should care for our bodies, in that we should not let them become polluted by sin. Better to limp through life than walk into hell. Our bodies are temples of the Holy Spirit and members of the Lord Jesus. This gives a tremendous significance to our life in the body.

In Leviticus, God's people were warned, 'Do not cut your bodies for the dead or put tattoo marks on yourselves. I am the LORD' (*Lev.* 19:28). Few are aware that primitive tattooing can have a religious meaning. Many races of the Pacific regard tattooing as an aid to the recipient in his passage through the underworld.

According to church historian Philip Schaff, among the reasons for the early church's conquest of the pagan world was its 'decency to the human body', in showing tender care for the dead. Julian the Apostate (332–363) regarded Christian care of the dead as one of the three factors accounting for its rapid spread after the first three centuries of persecution. The other two were the Christians' love for one another and their honesty.

Like the Jews, Christians washed and wrapped the dead body (as was done with Christ) before placing it in the earth. Occasionally the body was embalmed. The catacombs are evidence of widespread care for the body after death.

Modern Jewry has continued with a reverence for the body. Rabbi Brasch, an authority on Jewish tradition, has written:

> When a Jew dies, the body is never left alone. This is now a sign of reverence . . . if a near-relative is unable to stay, special 'watchers' consider it a privilege and a sacred duty to do so. Funeral arrangements are taken care of by the 'The Holy Brotherhood' (known by its Aramaic name of *Chevra Kadisha*). The members of this brotherhood are the most pious of the Jewish community who know that to pay the last respect to the dead is one of the great religious duties of man. They do so, not in mere words or gestures, but by actually preparing the body for the last rest, washing and clothing it. They give their service readily to every Jew as though he were a brother, because in death each is a king and no one a stranger. Complete simplicity and equality distinguish Jewish burial. The coffin itself must be of the simplest kind, unvarnished and unadorned. In no circumstances is it permitted to differentiate between the rich and the poor, the 'famous' and the 'ordinary'.[1]

Since Jews still have such a high view of the body, how much more should Christians, in the light of the resurrection of our Lord.

John Murray reminds us that, even in death, the body that is laid in the tomb is not simply a body:

> It is the body of the person. More properly, it is the person as respects the body. It is the person who is buried or laid in the tomb. How eloquent of this is the usage respecting our Lord.

[1] Cited by Philip Oliver in 'The Christian Way of Death', *Australian Church Record*, June 1972.

He was buried. He rose from the dead. In reference to Jesus the angel said, 'Come and see the place where he lay.' Jesus also said, 'All that are in the graves will hear his voice.' To Lazarus he said, 'Lazarus, come forth.' Believers are dead in Christ, they sleep through Jesus. So what is laid in the grave is still integral to the person who died. In and during death, the person is identified with the dissolved material entity. This underlies the gravity of death and the return to dust. 'To dust *thou* shalt return', as also 'Dust *thou* art.'[1]

It was in the body that we knew and loved those whom we lay to rest. We have to ask ourselves how we should treat the body in order that our love might be constant in death as life. By our treatment of our dead we should ensure that the dignity of the divinely-created body is upheld to its earthly end. The dissolution of the body is not a natural process which we are at liberty to hasten or delay at will. It is the punishment which God has inflicted upon sin (*Gen.* 3:19).

The Need to Grieve

Grief is an experience common to all. It is not only associated with death, but whatever the reason its symptoms show themselves to a greater or lesser degree.[2]

A feature of Jewish funeral procedure is the opportunity to express grief. After the burial, family members stay at home and 'sit shivah' for seven days. This is a period of deep mourning with regular prayers. They may wear some torn cloth as a symbol of the traditional 'shredded garment'; they may keep an unkempt appearance; friends will bring food to indicate the inability of the bereaved to concern themselves with practical affairs.

[1] *Collected Writings*, vol.2, Edinburgh: Banner of Truth, 1977, p. 16.
[2] See the author's booklet *Christians Grieve Too*, also published by the Banner of Truth Trust.

How different from the practice more or less regarded as the norm for most Christian funerals! Elaborate coffins, magnificent funeral 'homes', expensive vehicles – all in stark contrast with the biblical simplicity observed by the Jews.

Professor Harry W. Martin of Texas Southwestern Medical School has deplored the 'slick, smooth operation' so frequent today. He questions the effect of 'saying no to weeping and wailing and expressing grief and loneliness . . . It may mean the we have to mourn covertly, by subterfuge – perhaps in various degrees of depression, perhaps in mad flights of activity, perhaps in booze.'[1]

Apart from some country areas where male mourners still join in shovelling earth to fill the grave, the undertaker today either puffs some dust or drops petals when 'earth to earth' is mentioned. As soon as possible, artificial lawn mats cover the grim reality of the site and the grave is filled after the mourners have left.

The rattle of clods on the coffin certainly provokes grief in what might seem a brutal fashion, but grief so expressed can hasten the healing of inner feelings more than denial or postponement of what is a natural and necessary emotion.

Psychologists have been expressing doubt for years about the abandonment of traditional forms of mourning. Nearly twenty years ago, an anthropologist named Gorer wrote on 'Death, Grief and Mourning'. He warned that modern services could result in 'callousness, irrational preoccupation with and fear of death'.[2]

Writing in *Newsweek* magazine, French social historian Philippe Aries reviewed burial practices over two thousand years. In the early period, Western man accepted death as

[1] *Time* magazine, 12 November 1965, p. 33.
[2] *Ibid*. p. 35.

his familiar, ordinary and expected destiny. Subtle modifications entered during the Middle Ages, death becoming more an individual experience than a common destiny, with families avoiding references to impending death in the hearing of the dying person. By the mid-twentieth century, death was rapidly disappearing from public view in the industrialized Western nations. Aries saw the increasing popularity of cremation as a confirmation of his opinion that the 'the once familiar face of death has become, in Western societies, something shameful and forbidden'.[1]

The more we reduce the impact of death and the opportunity to grieve, the more psychological complications tend to arise over a longer period than we might normally expect. One of the reasons for the popularity of cremation is the brevity of the ceremony. This tends to 'short circuit' the expression of grief and can result in a complication of the later grieving process.

The service itself is rather anti-climactic. It is amazing how many people on their first visit to a crematorium service expect the coffin to pass directly into the furnace. Instead it either passes through a small door or is hidden by a curtain. This tends to camouflage the completeness of the separation which burial brings; there is a lack of finality.

Professor Graeme Griffin of the Uniting Church in Melbourne says cremation leaves fewer reminders of death. An Australian funeral director, writing in *Good Weekend* magazine, Sydney, found cremation 'much easier than a burial'. In a burial, 'If it's pouring with rain, people stand around and get thoroughly miserable.'

---

[1] *Newsweek* magazine, 1 May 1978, p. 41.

'Being miserable' in such a context might be a cathartic experience enabling the mourner better to cope with the reality of grief once the initial shock has worn off.

The disposal of the body is part – not all – of the healing process and needs to be considered against the background of grief.

Grief can be less burdensome where there is a tribute to the dead person's life. But this 'celebration of life' must not obscure the fact that the service is primarily due to death. So often the dead person's life (whether a Christian or not) can be misinterpreted as the basis for our eternal hope and not the finished work of Christ.

Planning for Death

Christians in particular should plan for their death. The 1662 *Book of Common Prayer* is brutally frank in the *Order for the Visitation of the Sick*. The minister is to 'examine (the sick person) whether he repent him truly of his sins, and be in charity with the world . . . let him be admonished to make his will . . .'

We might well add, 'and give thought to planning his funeral.'

Statements such as, 'I don't care what they do with me when I die' ought not to have any place in Christian thinking.[1] In death, as in life, we should seek to glorify our Lord and Saviour Jesus Christ. The body is God's creation; it is in the body that we remember our loved ones; it is in the body that they served him in life and it will be in a changed body that they shall be raised.

Holding this belief, we should treat the body with the same loving care as did the early church. We ought to seriously

[1] Oliver, 'The Christian Way of Death'.

[26]

consider emulating modern Jewish practice in the economy and uniformity of burial preparations.

The order of service, the hymns, the Bible readings, ought all to be discussed well before death with both family and minister.

A grand old saint in my congregation, having moved into his 90s, discussed his service with me. He was one of the few for whom I was able to take as a funeral text the words of Paul, 'I have fought a good fight, I have finished my course, I have kept the faith' (2 *Tim.* 4:17). For the final hymn, we chose 'Onward Christian Soldiers'. Some of the family queried its use, but they did not object. It was a grand climax to a service which stressed the sure hope of those who die in Christ – comforting to mourners, an encouragement to believers and a challenge to all.

Christians should recognize, as do the Jews, that an elaborate and costly coffin is not necessary for a dignified service. So often mourners are misled by their troubled emotions (perhaps by their conscience where there is cause for guilt) and lay out great sums of money for a container that will soon disintegrate in the flames or be hidden from view in the ground.

Apart from the expense, an elaborate moisture-proof casket (the euphemism favoured by undertakers for 'coffin'), and special vaults tend to obscure the reality that God's judgment is that dust we are and to dust we must eventually return.[1] It is interesting that the earthly remains of the great Reformation scholar John Calvin lie in an unmarked grave.

A few flowers in the church and a wreath on the coffin check dullness, but elaborate floral tributes are really a waste.

[1] Dr Norman Shepherd, in correspondence, *Banner of Truth*, April 1971, pp. 13–14.

Some families request donations for a charity in lieu of flowers, but is doubtful that many bother. The Gideons have a Memorial Bible Fund and willingly display sample Bibles at the service and provide blank cheque forms for donors to fill in.

If there is time, there is no reason why executors should not ask several undertakers for a quote before the final decision. It is questionable whether mourners' cars need to be hired when many friends will be happy to provide transport.

Why do we hesitate to take such a practical step as planning our funeral service? The reason is simple: although death is so certain, no one likes thinking about it.

Some years before his own death, D. Broughton Knox wrote:

> This shows that it is not part of God's design. We cannot understand death apart from what the Bible says about it, namely, that death is the consequence and penalty for sin and for rebellion and turning against God . . . Everyone of us, Christian or non-Christian, deserves this fate; but by calling on Jesus as Lord, we will escape it, for by the death of Christ, we have been redeemed from it. When we have been forgiven in Christ, death has lost its sting; for Christ has passed through it and risen triumphant over it. We should never think of death without thinking also of Jesus Christ the vanquisher of death.[1]

Since this is the Christian's sure hope, our last association with the body of one who has gone to be with the Lord should proclaim this truth.

Those who leave instructions for burial rather than for cremation know that their last link with family and friends

[1] *Australian Church Record*, 29 May 1975

will give vivid expression to the doctrine that what is sown shall one day be raised.

Some seek to testify to this truth by burying the ashes in a container. The problem is that the burning process is now so efficient that only about twenty per cent of the body (mostly bone) survives as ash. So often ashes are disposed of by sentiment – scattered at sea, in a rose garden, from an aircraft, and so on. In such instances there is no testimony to future resurrection.

Peter FitzSimons, a leading Australian rugby and sporting writer, wrote in his column in a Sydney paper that 'Canuck's Sportsman's Memorials' in the US insert the ashes of sports enthusiasts 'into the shafts of golf clubs, the centres of bowling balls or whatever sporting tool the family desires, and return them'. According to the proprietor, 'It's important for the loved ones to do something constructive with the remains.' FitzSimons made the laconic comment: 'He got that right.'[1] Others have blasted ashes into space via satellite, put them into fireworks and even placed them in beer cans. Such bizarre treatment may seem amusing, but disregards the dignity of the body.

Christian Burial

It is the high and holy privilege of the believer to be united to Jesus Christ both in life and in death.

In life, believers are 'in Christ': Jesus is the vine and believers are branches abiding in him and he in them (*John* 15:4). This union with Christ enables us to enjoy all the benefits which are ours through his life, death and resurrection. In death, believers are 'with Christ' – not even death can sever our relationship with him (Romans 8:38–39).

[1] *Sydney Morning Herald*, 8 November 1993

Since the bodies of believers belong to the Lord in death as much as in life, we need to ask whether we have the liberty to subject them to modern cremation.

God has declared the destruction of the body to be punishment for sin; its dissolution in the ground is unnatural; its turning to dust is the effect of his sentence.

Cremation certainly expedites the process, but the process in itself is violent. Incinerators in crematoria are fuelled by natural gas and destroy the body at a temperature between 800 and 1000 degrees Centigrade. Bones are then broken down in what is effectively a tumble dryer with large steel balls.[1]

Embalming is questionable as it aims to delay dissolution as long as possible. The same argument applies to freezing the body in the vain hope that one day it can be restored to life as medical science advances ('Cryonics').

'We should all look death fully in the face and realise that it is the reward of our sins,' wrote Broughton Knox. 'Grim though it is, it is merely an outward index of the much more awful darkness of complete separation from God, the source of all light. This is what we have brought on ourselves by our sins.'[2]

Physical death is a manifestation of the eternal separation which sin brings, but there is no condemnation for those who die in Christ Jesus (*Rom.* 8:1). Even in death we are able to proclaim the glorious truth that Jesus is the resurrection and the life. This truth should direct how our bodies are finally treated. The burial of the body gives explicit expression to the analogy of the seed sown resulting in a future harvest; it is a distinctive testimony to the future Christian hope of resurrection.

[1] *Sydney Morning Herald*, 8 November 1993.
[2] *Australian Church Record*, 29 May 1975

Although 'going to heaven' expresses a joyous truth of the Christian's security after death, Donald Robinson says that we should balance this expression with another much treasured by earlier generations: 'Expecting the resurrection' – for the earth, with all its quick and dead, awaits the coming of its Lord.[1]

Every activity and opinion of the Christian must be based upon Biblical premises. These include living and dying. As death is the last opportunity any of us will have to testify to God's truth, what is more fitting than that our passing should focus upon the unique and distinctive doctrine of the resurrection of the body?

My wife's maternal grandfather had a distinguished public career and was honoured by the Queen for his services. Cabinet ministers and community leaders attended his funeral and were sincere in their tributes. After most of the mourners had left the cemetery, we led our two small daughters to the grave of their beloved 'Pa', who had quoted John 3:16 shortly before he died.

The honorifics meant nothing to their young minds. All they knew was that the one they loved and who had loved them had gone from their lives. They looked down on the last earthly resting place of one who was a true patriarch; they dropped the little flowers they had taken from the wreaths and looked solemnly into the grave while we gently explained the Christian hope. It was a simple and moving way for us to express our feelings and we hope that the memory remains with our children until the end of their earthly pilgrimage.

---

[1] D. W. B. Robinson, *The Hope of Christ's Coming*, Beecroft, N.S.W.: Evangelical Tracts and Publications, 1958, p. 22

How final it was, as far as the ties that bind us on earth are concerned! How peaceful the scene about us! Such feelings could never have been expressed over a body given for burning.

Of course, this may be speaking sentimentally rather than theologically, but emotions are important and it was a precious experience for us all.

Said F. D. Maurice:

> The more I think of the way in which the children of Israel asserted their right to the possession of Canaan, in which they had not one foot of other ground, merely by burying their dead in it . . . the more do I feel that every body put into this earth is a new invasion of Satan's present dominion, a new declaration that Christ is coming to claim the earth for His Church.[1]

'The earth is the LORD's and the fullness thereof; the world and they that dwell therein!' (*Psa.* 24:1).

'He who testifies to these things says, 'Yes, I am coming soon.'

'Amen, Come, Lord Jesus!' (*Rev.* 22:20).

---

[1] Cited by D. W. B. Robinson in *The Hope of Christ's Coming*.